Landforms
CANYONS

by Sonja Olson

FOCUS
READERS

www.focusreaders.com

Focus Readers is distributed by North Star Editions:
sales@northstareditions.com | 888-417-0195

Produced for Focus Readers by Red Line Editorial.

Photographs ©: sumikophoto/Shutterstock Images, cover, 1; livetalent/iStockphoto, 4–5; GoodLifeStudio/iStockphoto, 6; Jonathan A. Mauer/Shutterstock Images, 8–9; luq1/iStockphoto, 10; Benjamin Simeneta/Shutterstock Images, 12; GitoTrevisan/iStockphoto, 14–15; Jacek_Sopotnicki/iStockphoto, 16, 29; InnaVar/Shutterstock Images, 19; MundusImages/iStockphoto, 20–21; mandj98/iStockphoto, 22–23; GeorgePeters/iStockphoto, 25; Trevor Sachs/iStockphoto, 27

ISBN
978-1-63517-890-6 (hardcover)
978-1-63517-991-0 (paperback)
978-1-64185-194-7 (ebook pdf)
978-1-64185-093-3 (hosted ebook)

Library of Congress Control Number: 2018931703

Printed in the United States of America
Mankato, MN
May, 2018

About the Author

Sonja Olson obtained her bachelor of fine arts in sculpture from the College of Visual Arts and a master's in curriculum and instruction from the University of Saint Thomas. Prone to rescue stray cats, Olson currently teaches, writes, creates, and resides in Saint Paul, Minnesota.

TABLE OF CONTENTS

CHAPTER 1

A DARK AND WINDING PATH

A long, jagged cut runs along the ground. It looks like a crack in the earth. The cut is deep. The sides are steep. Rocks cast shadows on the ground. Sunlight cannot reach the bottom of the canyon.

 The Siq is a canyon in Jordan.

 A canyon's walls are like steep cliffs.

A canyon is a deep cut in the earth. In some places, the sides of a canyon are rough. In other places, the sides are smooth. Often a river is at the bottom.

Canyons can be found all over the world. They are often in dry, hot areas. But they can also be underwater. Canyons can even be found on other planets.

FUN FACT

The largest known canyon is on Mars. The canyon is as long as the United States.

CHAPTER 2

WATER IS A MIGHTY FORCE

Canyons exist because of water. The movement of water causes **erosion**. As the rock wears away, a canyon forms. But a canyon does not form quickly. It can take millions of years.

 Many canyons are formed when a river erodes rock.

Over time, even small rivers can make deep cuts in a plateau.

There are several types of canyons. One type is known as a **plateau** canyon. Over many years, a river can erode the plateau.

This process forms a wide, V-shaped canyon.

Flash floods can make slot canyons. Slot canyons are deep and narrow. In a flash flood, a lot of water comes into an area. This moving water can erode the rock. Over time, a canyon forms.

FUN FACT

The deepest canyon on Earth is the Tsangpo Canyon in China. Some sections are more than 17,000 feet (5,000 m) deep.

 Antelope Canyon in Arizona is a slot canyon.

Flood water can also run into

cracks in the rock. If the water

12

freezes, it expands. This can break the rocks apart. This process can create slot canyons as well.

Canyons can be underwater, too. These canyons are often found where a river meets the ocean. This happens at the outer edge of a continent. The river's **current** makes the water move. The water pours into the ocean. It flows over the **continental shelf**. The current erodes the ocean floor. Over time, a **submarine** canyon forms.

CHAPTER 3

VISUAL HISTORY

Canyons are made up of many layers of rock. Each layer formed at a different time. The lowest layers are the oldest. The highest layers are the youngest. Each layer formed in different conditions.

 Rock layers take many years to form.

 Rock layers show scientists how a canyon has changed over time.

Some layers may have formed when the climate was wet. Other layers may have formed when the climate was dry. Scientists study them carefully. They learn how the climate has changed over time.

Canyons also help scientists learn about **ancient** animals. When animals die, they may become **fossils**. When a new fossil is found, scientists study the rock around it. The age of this rock can help determine the age of the fossil.

FUN FACT

Fish River Canyon is in Africa. Parts of the canyon are 1,800 feet (550 m) deep. The deepest rocks are more than two billion years old. The highest rocks are 200 to 550 million years old.

Other fossils in the same layer are the same age. This helps scientists learn what animals were alive at the same time.

Canyons change very slowly. But erosion is always happening. A canyon's layers may show patterns

FUN FACT

Red Rock Canyon is in California. It has fossils that are eight to twelve million years old. These include bones from **extinct** elephants, saber-toothed cats, and ancient alligators.

 Erosion helped make some of the fossils in Red Rock Canyon visible.

in erosion. The patterns can help scientists predict what the canyon will look like in the future.

THE GRAND CANYON

The Grand Canyon is in Arizona. Scientists believe it began forming more than two billion years ago. The Colorado River carved the canyon over many years. The Grand Canyon erodes approximately 1 foot (0.3 m) every 200 years.

Today, the Grand Canyon is home to more than 1,500 types of plants. More than 500 kinds of animals live there, too. One is the California condor. This bird is rare and endangered. Scientists raise baby condors to release into the wild. In this way, they try to prevent condors from becoming extinct.

The Grand Canyon is a plateau canyon.

CHAPTER 4

LAYERS OF LIFE

Canyons are often in dry areas. But the **environment** inside a canyon varies. The top of a canyon is warmer than the bottom. It gets light from the sun. This area has the most animals and plants.

A bighorn sheep looks over the edge of the Grand Canyon.

The deeper parts are cooler. These parts are darker, too. They do not get much light. Some plants and animals can live here. But these animals do not need as much sunlight to survive.

Canyons are home to a wide variety of life. Many amphibians and

FUN FACT

People also live in or near canyons. There is evidence of human life in the Grand Canyon from as early as 13,000 years ago.

 The rivers at the base of many canyons provide water for plants and animals.

reptiles live in canyons. Fish live in the rivers at the bottom. Birds often live near the top of a canyon.

Bighorn sheep have special hooves they use to climb the rocky sides. Coyotes and mountain lions prowl canyons, too. Cacti, ferns, and wildflowers all grow in different areas.

Submarine canyons have different wildlife. Fish and eels can be

FUN FACT

Scientists use underwater vehicles to explore submarine canyons. These vehicles have helped scientists discover many new kinds of sea creatures.

 Anemones in submarine canyons can provide homes for certain kinds of fish.

found in these canyons. Algae and

water plants grow on the rocks.

Anemones and corals live there

as well.

FOCUS ON
CANYONS

Write your answers on a separate piece of paper.

1. Write a paragraph describing how water can create a canyon.

2. What type of canyon would you like to explore? Why?

3. What is the name of a canyon that forms underwater?
   - **A.** plateau canyon
   - **B.** slot canyon
   - **C.** submarine canyon

4. What could scientists know if they found fossils of two animals in the same layer of rock?
   - **A.** The animals ate the same food.
   - **B.** The animals lived at the same time.
   - **C.** The animals lived at different times.

5. What does **jagged** mean in this book?

*A long, **jagged** cut runs along the ground. It looks like a crack in the earth.*

    A. having uneven edges
    B. having smooth edges
    C. having no edges

6. What does **predict** mean in this book?

*The patterns can help scientists **predict** what the canyon will look like in the future.*

    A. to change what is happening
    B. to make a guess about what will happen
    C. to study what happened in the past

Answer key on page 32.

GLOSSARY

ancient
Very old.

continental shelf
An underwater slope at the edge of a continent.

current
A water movement that goes in a certain direction.

environment
Everything that surrounds and affects a living thing.

erosion
The act of wearing away a surface.

extinct
No longer living on Earth.

flash floods
Sudden rushes of water caused by heavy rain.

fossils
Parts of an animal or plant that remain preserved in rock.

plateau
A high area of land with a flat surface.

submarine
Deep underwater.

TO LEARN MORE

BOOKS

Chin, Jason. *Grand Canyon*. New York: Roaring Brook Press, 2017.

Gregory, Josh. *Grand Canyon*. New York: Scholastic, 2018.

Rector, Rebecca Kraft. *The Grand Canyon*. Lake Elmo, MN: Focus Readers, 2018.

NOTE TO EDUCATORS

Visit **www.focusreaders.com** to find lesson plans, activities, links, and other resources related to this title.

INDEX

Answer Key: 1. Answers will vary; **2.** Answers will vary; **3.** C; **4.** B; **5.** A; **6.** B